T0353847

SOMEWHERE IN THE LAND OF NOWHERE

JANE MARRINER

AuthorHouse™ UK
1663 Liberty Drive
Bloomington, IN 47403 USA
www.authorhouse.co.uk
UK TFN: 0800 0148641 (Toll Free inside the UK)
UK Local: 02036 956322 (+44 20 3695 6322 from outside the UK)

Because of the dynamic nature of the Internet, any web addresses or links contained in this book may have changed since publication and may no longer be valid. The views expressed in this work are solely those of the author and do not necessarily reflect the views of the publisher, and the publisher hereby disclaims any responsibility for them.

Any people depicted in stock imagery provided by Getty Images are models, and such images are being used for illustrative purposes only. Certain stock imagery © Getty Images.

This book is printed on acid-free paper.

ISBN: 979-8-8230-8869-5 (sc)
ISBN: 979-8-8230-8870-1 (e)

Library of Congress Control Number: 2024914345

Print information available on the last page.

Published by AuthorHouse 07/11/2024

authorHOUSE

SOMEWHERE IN THE LAND OF NOWHERE

Somewhere in the Land of Nowhere, stood two rocky mountains with a stream which gushed and gurgled between them.

At the base of one mountain, there was a spacious burrow in which lived Ribett Rabbit, Becky Bird and Hamish Hedgehog. Also, there was Bouncy Bean who could forecast the weather by changing his colour. Ribett Rabbit wore a fez on his head with holes for his ears to peep through. Becky Bird boasted a crest of lustrous feathers which she could raise at will. Hamish Hedgehog wore spines tipped with spiky balls.

Ribett Rabbit tended to a vegetable tree, a fruity fruit tree, a cup cake tree, and a sugar coated sweetie tree. Hamish Hedgehog and Becky Bird fed off slugs and snails around the trees thus saving the trees from damage.

At the top of the mountain was a deep cavern carved into the rocks. It was home to the Gabbygobbies, who chattered and chortled through their wide mouths.

Father Gabbygobbie grew a curl at the centre of his flat head. Mother Gabbygobbie fashioned large brimmed hats from grasses growing between the rocks. These protected them all from the hot sun and the heavy rain.

Baby Gabbygobbie sat atop Mother Gabbygobbie's flat head, while he tried unsuccessfully to catch the butterflies fluttering by.

The Gabbygobbies came down the mountain to buy Ribett Rabbit's vegetables, fruity fruit, cup cakes and sweeties. They placed them all in their upturned hats, leaving their strong long arms and legs to help themselves climb back up the mountain to their cosy cavern.

Built into the far side of this mountain was a store which offered groceries, and all manner of domestic items and tools. The owner was Jolly Ginger Jimbo who sported a ginger moustache. He wore a long ginger coat with numerous pockets in which he deposited bits and pieces from his store.

His friend was a dog named Gannet who loved to eat large quantities of all sorts of food. Gannet Dog liked to show off his strong tail which he swished menacingly at anyone who annoyed him.

Jolly Ginger Jimbo kept a hot air balloon at the back of the store which he took out at weekends and holidays. He had massive lungs, and was able to stand in the middle of the balloon's basket. He was then able to breathe out great gusts of air to inflate the balloon's canopy. Jolly Ginger Jimbo was very proud of this ability, which of course used no gas to pollute the atmosphere in which he flew his hot air balloon.

Ribett Rabbit, Hamish Hedgehog, Becky Bird, Bouncy Bean, and the Gabbygobbies accompanied Jolly Ginger Jimbo and Gannet Dog. They enjoyed many hot air balloon trips, across the skies, high above the mountains where they could view the scenery below.

The other mountain stood on the far side of the stream, where the family of Gongoes resided in a vast tunnel stretching far into the mountain.

The Gongoe family had eyes on top of their heads, and extremely large feet. They pounded up and down the vast tunnel, making a noise which echoed around the mountain. The Gongoes dined mainly on rabbit stew.

Rabbits who made the mistake of straying too near the tunnel were invited inside. The Gongoes then tempted them with a secret potion, which sent them to sleep. Father Gongoe then picked them up, and dropped them into a large metal cauldron, simmering on an open fire.

Father Gongoe wore a belt of rabbit's tails or scuts as they are properly named. Mother Gongoe swung a string of rabbit scuts round her neck, which she had dyed red, to match the nail polish on her large toes.

Baby Gongoe had a pearl slide in her hair. She wasn't very fond of rabbit stew, so she made friends with Ribett Rabbit on the other mountain. He often gave her cup cakes and sweeties from his trees.

The climate was changing in the Land of Nowhere. The mountain residents had to adapt to sudden storms, fierce winds, driving rain, and spells of exhaustingly hot weather.

One day, Bouncy Bean awoke in the burrow in an agitated state.

"Look at me, Ribett Rabbit. Look at me, Becky Bird. Look at me, Hamish Hedgehog!" They all looked, and saw that Bouncy Bean had turned a deep purple colour.

"A ferocious storm is coming, we must warn Jolly Ginger Jimbo and Gannet Dog," Bouncy Bean declared.

They all helped Jolly Ginger Jimbo to stack as many goods as possible onto the highest shelves in the store.

However,when the storm arrived, it frightened everybody, with lightening and heavy rain. The stream between the mountains became a raging torrent, flooding the floor of the store, and sweeping items out of the door and far away.

Ribett Rabbit, Gannet Dog, and Jolly Ginger Jimbo managed to scramble on top of a big table, before that also sailed down the swollen stream.

Becky Bird perched on Ribett Rabbit's fez, shrieking distressfully. Bouncy Bean bounced about on Gannet Dog's back.

Then with one voice, they all exclaimed "Where is Hamish Hedgehog where has he gone!"

Meanwhile, the Gabbygobbies peeped out of their cavern, gripping their hats to their flat heads. They were promptly blown down to the bottom of the mountain, where they clutched at whatever prevented themselves from falling into the surging water.

Suddenly, Baby Gabbygobbie shouted out "I can see Hamish Hedgehog hurtling through the waves towards us." Just as Hamish Hedgehog was being swept past them, Father Gabbygobbie pulled off his hat. Grasping the wide brim tightly, he waved it in front of Hamish Hedgehog, who tumbled in, and was hauled safely onto the rocks.

"Thank you, thank you" whispered Hamish Hedgehog, who could barely talk, so shocked was he, after his ordeal.

The big table got caught in a branch bending over the water. Luckily, Ribett Rabbit, Gannet Dog and Jolly Ginger Jimbo were able to clamber on to the mountain side. Bouncy Bean bounced, and Becky Bird fluttered to safety with them.

The Gongoe family sensibly pounded to the far end of their tunnel, where they sat singing songs together until the storm had abated.

Following the storm, all the goods in the store were restored to their former places.

Ribett Rabbit was relieved to see that the vegetable tree, the fruity fruit tree, the cup cake tree, and the sugar coated sweetie tree had all survived the storm. Of course, some vegetables, fruit, cup cakes and sweeties had been borne away on the gusty wind.

Sometime later, the sun decided to throw his hottest rays across the Land of Nowhere, scorching all the crops on the ground. This enraged a swarm of locusts searching for food.

"Aha," the locust leader chirped. "I spy Ribett Rabbit's trees. They will satisfy our appetites wonderfully."

The trees were quickly stripped, and were left leaning forlornly towards each other in a very sorry state.

Jolly Ginger Jimbo reached for his hot air balloon which was undamaged, fortunately. He, and Gannet Dog filled it with all the groceries from the store. Then they guided the hot air balloon round to the burrow delivering provisions to the occupants waiting there, who were most grateful. The hot air balloon was then flown to the top of the mountain with the remainder of the groceries for the Gabbygobbies who thanked Jolly Ginger Jimbo for his kindness.

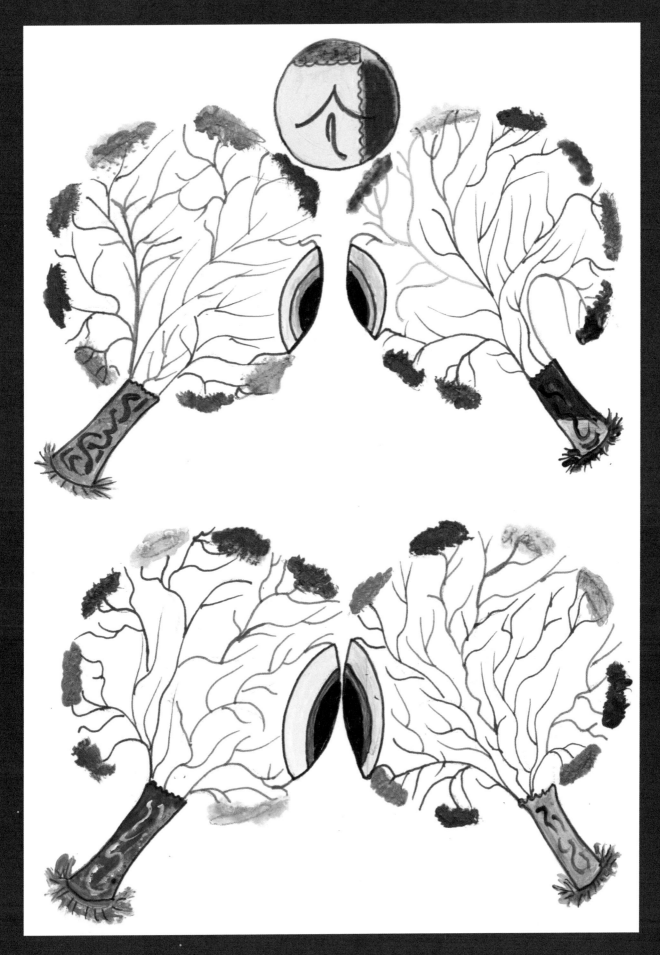

Next day, everyone climbed into the hot air balloon in order to survey the scenery from the skies, and to see what damage the storm had wreaked.

As Jolly Ginger Jimbo was about to bring the hot air balloon back down, a mean and mighty gust of wind ripped through the canopy. The hot air balloon was flung across the stream to the other mountain, and became entangled round a large rock. Everyone was thrown out, and sat dazed and disorientated on the mountain side.

The Gongoe family sped down the mountain to offer their help, and lead the way to their tunnel home.

All were offered rabbit stew, which was politely refused. Father Gabbygobbie glanced at a shaking Ribett Rabbit, and suddenly they all realized how much danger Ribett Rabbit was in.

"We must leave now, and return to the hot air balloon," said Mother Gabbygobbie.

"Perhaps Ribett Rabbit would enjoy a tumbler of our special drink, he looks thirsty," suggested Father Gongoe.

"No,no,no!" they all chorused, rushing back down the tunnel.

Father Gongoe lunged at poor Ribett Rabbit, but Baby Gongoe was too fast for him. Remembering Ribett Rabbit giving her sweeties and cupcakes from his trees, she caught his arm.

"Quick, quick, we must take my secret path to the base of the mountain."

So, they both vanished, leaving an angry Father and Mother Gongoe to pursue the others.

Jolly Ginger Jimbo pulled an enormous hammer from one of his numerous coat pockets.

As he fled past the rabbit stew cauldron, he struck it as hard as he was able. The cauldron tipped over and rolled down the mountain. Mother Gabbygobbie fanned the open fire used to cook the rabbit stew with her wide brimmed hat, until the flames died away.

Mother Gongoe was just behind her, but stumbled on Hamish Hedgehog. He dug his spines tipped with spiky balls deep into her extremely large feet, causing her to cry out in pain. Bouncy Bean jumped up and down between her eyes and across her head. Mother Gongoe gave up the chase, and crawled back to the safety of the tunnel.

Father Gongoe was still racing after Jolly Ginger Jimbo, who was shooting peas at him from a pea shooter taken from another coat pocket.

Gannet Dog charged in front of Father Gongoe and whipped his strong tail across Father Gongoe's legs, making him fall over.

Becky Bird raised her lustrous feather crest. It caught the sun's rays, dazzling Father Gongoe so much, that he could no longer see clearly.

Jolly Ginger Jimbo took hold of Father Gongoe's shoulders, and shook him so violently that all his teeth fell out.

"If I hear of you ever harming another rabbit, I will push YOU into a hot cauldron!" shouted Jolly Ginger Jimbo into Father Gongoe's ear.

Father Gongoe nodded in defeat, and was left to ponder on his misfortune.

Baby Gongoe and Ribett Rabbit came round the rocks, and were united with the others, and there were lots of hugs and kisses.

Ribett Rabbit thanked Baby Gongoe for her help, and they waved goodbye, promising to

meet again shortly.

Jolly Ginger Jimbo repaired the hot air balloon with yet more tools from his array of coat pockets. Eventually, everyone hopped into the basket and returned to their own mountain.

Soon, the trees started producing more vegetables, fruity fruits, cup cakes and sweeties than ever before.

Becky Bird and Hamish Hedgehog continued their meals of slugs and snails.

Jolly Ginger Jimbo delighted in taking everyone for hot air balloon rides again.

There were no further mishaps, and life was enjoyed by all once more.

Printed in the United States
by Baker & Taylor Publisher Services